Managing Information

in a week

Bob Norton

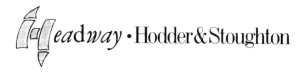

Headway · Hodder & Stoughton

British Library Cataloguing in Publication Data
A catalogue record for this title is available from the British
Library

ISBN 0 340 63153 8

First published 1995
Impression number 10 9 8 7 6 5 4 3 2 1
Year   1999 1998 1997 1996 1995

Typeset by Multiplex Techniques Ltd, Orpington, Kent.
Printed in Great Britain for Hodder & Stoughton
Educational, a division of Hodder Headline Plc,
338 Euston Road, London NW1 3BH
by St Edmundsbury Press, Bury St Edmunds Suffolk.

the *Institute*
of Management

FOUNDATION

The Institute of Management (IM) is at the forefront of management development and best management practice. The Institute embraces all levels of management from students to chief executives. It provides a unique portfolio of services for all managers, enabling them to develop skills and achieve management excellence.

For information on the benefits of membership, please write to:

Department HS
Institute of Management
Cottingham Road
Corby
Northants NN17 1TT
Tel. 01536 204222
Fax 01536 201651

This series is commissioned by the Institute of Management Foundation.

C O N T E N T S

Information can be a boon or a bane. We all need it but most of us let it get the better of us by having too much, or not enough and in the wrong time and place.

Today information is the bread and butter of business. The key to success is to apply it with the right pressure in the right quantity at the right place and time. We then get the quality we want.

Managing Information in a Week offers a practical route through the information maze with methods and guidance which can help to improve control, save time, increase effectiveness and explore new techniques.

We will look at:

Sunday	Using information in the product life cycle
Monday	Planning and organisation
Tuesday	Searching and evaluation
Wednesday	Storage and retrieval procedures
Thursday	Delivering information
Friday	Putting information to use
Saturday	Legal constraints

Thus, *Managing Information in a Week* offers a framework for understanding and controlling many of the processes through which information passes, and simple guidelines for exploiting it to maximum advantage. Remember, information is **power**, but its value depends very much on the use to which it is put.

Information use in the product life cycle

Today we start by looking at how information is put to use in the product life cycle. First, however, we need to define exactly what we mean by 'information'.

Defining information

Information, like beauty, depends on the eye of the beholder. It has no intrinsic value in itself; value is conferred by the user. Until that happens, what we have is no more than raw data: ideas, facts or figures, a book on the shelf, an article in a journal, a statistic on the page, even a picture on the wall. These then need to be sorted and manipulated to turn data into useable information. But information is not knowledge or intelligence, just halfway to it. To convert information into intelligence, we need to analyse, interpret and apply it in order to solve problems, make decisions or draw conclusions.

The product life cycle

The product life cycle provides a framework for developing, testing, designing, promoting and maintaining a new product or service. It also illustrates how the right information at the right time can be exploited beneficially in the many contexts and applications of the workplace.

Stages in the product life cycle
1   Ideas: a product or service has to begin
    somewhere
2   Screening: testing ideas for practicality

Although the use of commercial databases is widely suggested throughout the following stages, it would be prejudicial to pick one or two from the many thousands increasingly available either on-line through telephone or data networks, or on CD-ROM. Some may, in certain subject areas, be self-selecting but the key is to choose with care according to particular needs. Selection aids are listed at the end of Tuesday.

1 *Generation of ideas*

Past studies have shown that many possible ideas for a new product or service will fail as they pass through the various development phases. To convert ideas into viable products or services is the function of this planned cycle. At this stage, the purpose is to think positively and imaginatively; critical examination comes later.

The generation of ideas can lean heavily on the technique of brainstorming for which there are a number of key factors.

- A worthwhile purpose and a clear objective
- An environment which engenders creativity
- An atmosphere free from diktat and criticism
- Encouragement to risk, share, and build ideas
- Avoidance of negative reaction
- Freedom of expression even for the impractical
- The attendance of those who can contribute

The emphasis is on creativity and on coming up with possible, not just probable, ideas. The time for criticism, evaluation and selection comes later when the creative process is completed.

Linking several facts or pieces of data can stimulate new thought processes. One organisation may create a better environment for the free exchange of information and ideas than another; much will depend on its culture and approach to learning and development. Those organisations employing continuous improvement techniques in quality or development schemes could well be a step ahead in this area.

Another key element in the generation of ideas is the systematic use of information. Regular scanning of journals and newspapers or databases of new products, market announcements, trade advertising and competitors' or funders' press releases can all help in the creation of new ideas, or the adaptation of old ones.

2 Screening

Screening involves pitching new ideas against the organisation's objectives and targets. Many organisations may not have clear objectives, but if we don't know where we are trying to go, we will have little hope of knowing how to get there.

Product strategy, which information feeds, must be compatible with overall corporate strategy. Identifying opportunities may require support from information sources, but it is already at this stage that the idea mortality rate begins with questions such as:

- What is the basic idea behind this?
- Does it fit with objectives and targets?
- What benefits does it offer?
- How might the idea be applied?
- How can we combine this with something we already do?
- What market opportunities does it offer?
- Will its costs outweigh its benefits?

Some ideas will be more practical than others; hopefully some will survive to the third phase.

3 *Market analysis*

Researching market needs and opportunities is the classic domain of information gathering and analysis. This is the area which can benefit from the integrated information technologies which bring together documents from different sources to produce new information. Much of this phase may well involve new work and new research. However, the use of existing market databases, in either electronic or hard-copy form can be invaluable in picking out demographic, social, economic and product trends, and in providing leads on potential customer segments by age, sex and socioeconomic grouping, by employment or education, or by disposable income.

The results of surveys and market-place studies undertaken by other organisations are increasingly available on databases and provide information on market shares and positions and industrial developments.

Successful market analysis depends on the use of both

internally generated information and that which can be
gleaned from published sources. In combining information
from diverse sources, the following questions are central:

- What is our primary market?
- What are the major segments of this market?
- What do we know about our customers?
- How do our customers see us?
- Do we know what our customers want?
- What kind of data is available on market segments?
- Are further markets suitable for penetration?
- Which new products or services are emerging?
- How are markets likely to change in the future?
- What do we know about the competition?

4 *Competitor analysis*

We will need to retrieve and analyse the market position
and balance sheets of the major players in, or emerging in,
the market. The first thing is to identify if there is a market
leader and why.

A wealth of company information is readily available on potential competitors or collaborators, as well as on customers and suppliers.

Company data
- Income and expenditure, reserves and debt
- Bankers and credit ratings
- International associates and subsidiaries
- Performance as reported in the press
- Performance as analysed in reports
- Products, senior executives and shareholders

All of this is public information – if it is a public company. Caveat: The smaller the company to be investigated, the less likely it is that published information will be readily available.

5   *Research and development*

If the idea has survived and matured so far, the successful design and development of our new product will require information from both business and technical databases. In determining the originality and feasibility of a new product, databases of scientific research and patents will be important. Environmental and legal implications may be researched in law and technical databases.

The major element in R & D is the contribution of appropriate specialists. Whether they work in chemical, physical, biological, engineering or other fields, databases, as the most effective method of controlling the masses of information available, exist to support them.

6   Testing

'The profile of your best customer is the profile of your best prospect.'

We may be fortunate enough to have recourse to an existing customer database on which we can draw to sample the new product.

If not, we can try to identify suitable customers to test the product by searching company databases by region, postcode, Standard Industrial Classification (SIC) code, turnover, or number of employees, in an attempt to find a wider-ranging sample than local panels or passer-by interviews may produce.

Many organisations have combined their own customer databases with purchased lists using specialist mailing-list software which integrates and de-duplicates. This is also an application for relational database systems which can merge data from different sources to provide a tool of powerful marketing potential. Caveat: It may prove to be a nightmare to update.

7   Product introduction

The four Ps – product, price, place and promotion – will need a fifth: planning. Databases can again provide much help with forecasting the likely market share and position, helping to assess uniqueness and value compared to other products, and to select distribution channels, packaging, brand-naming and promotional techniques. Marketing and management databases can not only provide us with ideas for strategies and techniques but also with case-studies of the success or failures of others. Learning best practice is often no more than studying the pain of trial and error of others.

8 *Production and logistics*

Information technology (IT) has combined these two major operations in the life-cycle process in response to the demands of the rapidly changing market and requirements for more timely delivery, shorter warehousing periods and cost cutting.

By their nature, production control systems use internally generated data. Using IT to link production to logistics, stock holdings have been reduced, and the efficiency of distribution has been revolutionised. In the past five years, a number of manufacturing systems have been developed in the USA which can convert from computer design to solid replica in days rather than weeks or months.

Engineering databases can provide the technical methods, and management databases the case-studies, of successful and unsuccessful applications of production and stock-control techniques such as:

- Kanban
- Just in time
- Lean production
- Simultaneous engineering
- Fast-track development

9   *Product growth and maturity*

It is a safe bet that competition and consumer familiarity
will erode the uniqueness of anything new in double-quick
time. Management control and effectiveness are vital to turn
an off-the-shelf commodity back into what was once an
original and premium-priced product or service. What is
lost as a product becomes established may, however, be
regained by tracking market developments in those same
databases used for development. Monitoring competitive
research and market launches is as much a feature of
maintenance as development. Further distribution channels
can be exploited with directory databases. We may find
innovative promotion techniques and update our skills,
ideas or methods through the creative use of management
and marketing databases.

Questions for management databases
- The pitfalls, as well as advantages, of TQM
- Real empowerment in a flatter organisation
- Approaches to successful teambuilding
- 'Intrapreneurship' in the organisation
- Successes of business re-engineering
- How to become a learning organisation
- How can we introduce benchmarking?
- The disadvantages of outsourcing

10 *Management development*

Personal effectiveness and development and the need to update skills are now of overriding importance to individual and organisational successes. Interest in the notion of competence as a measurement of ability and output, as opposed to learning, has grown rapidly. New flexible management development programmes have now begun to replace traditional skill-based short course programmes, where, in the sad past, Fred was sent on a two-day course once a year to make the training records look acceptable. Adaptable programmes have evolved around the core competences dealing with people, finance, operations and information to cater for a wide variety of development needs, and different styles and paces of learning.

Databases of films, videos and computer-based training packages now complement those covering books and journal articles. They can be used for finding out about the skills and techniques of:

- Presentation and public speaking
- Managing change and innovation
- Communication
- Motivation
- Handling stress
- Interviewing
- Pricing
- Risk management
- Negotiation skills

to name but a few among the many hundreds aspects of management.

These databases offer access to flexible self-development in a period when change is a constant and jobs are for months or years, no longer for life.

Summary

Today, we have looked at how information is put to use in the workplace through a sequence of development which occurs in most organisations, known as the product life cycle.

Checkpoint: Am I gaining benefit from the wealth of information sources available in developing or maintaining my product or service?

It is essential to remember that to get the best from the information available, we have to know what we are looking for, where to look and what questions to ask. The more the information there is, the easier it is to take the wrong road, or to get lost in the maze.

We also need to know how information systems backfire and go wrong so that we know what to avoid, and how people really use information, so that we can begin to get it right.

Tomorrow we tackle these problems and suggest some solutions.

Where do we start?

Today, we will illustrate why information systems may have been unsuccessful in the past and will try to fit information needs into a coherent framework for use. We shall look at information in a number of contexts:

- The wrong time and place
- The wrong person
- The wrong information
- Computers
- Information systems
- People
- Organisation culture
- The audit
- Information costing and value

The wrong time and place

First there are problems with the use of information which call its value into question; problems such as:

- Overload: too much information, delivered at the wrong time
- Digestibility: too much dross and delivered in the wrong form – 'non-information'
- Misdirection: delivered to the wrong person
- Suitability; the wrong person at the wrong time for the wrong use.

For some, the latest report of market intelligence on the yoghurt market in Switzerland may be wholly appropriate. For others, learning of a new bypass or a new piece of environmental legislation may be more vital. It all depends on what people are working on, and how, and when.

The wrong person

Within an organisation there are attitudes and approaches which can reduce or cancel the value of information for the recipient.

Attitudes and approaches
- Apparent priorities
- Fixed ideas
- Communication
- Operational framework

Apparent priorities
'I have no more time, I just have to get on with it.'
Objectively it is easy to criticise this attitude. However, in the context of the working day, this is the reality faced by many with challenging deadlines, and conflicting priorities. Added to that, gathering and analysing information can be amongst the most time-consuming of activities.

Attitude

'I've made up my mind; don't confuse me with the facts.'
This is equally widespread, even if not stated quite like this.
On the other hand it is a whole lot less defensible. The
manager with fixed, preconceived ideas can do as much
damage as the one who will not risk a change of direction
for fear of being seen to be weak and inconsistent.
Information use should lead to contingency planning and
alternatives.

Communication

'I'm afraid I didn't understand it quite like that.' If everyone
is an information manager, then everyone is certainly a
communicator. Whilst lack of the right information at the
right time probably accounts for many howlers,
misunderstandings will account for many more. Perhaps the
two are the same. For example, ask 10 people what
'information' is and you will get 10 different answers.

Operational framework
'I'm afraid this just doesn't fit with the rest of my information'. If managers base their decisions only on information that 'fits' an understood pattern as opposed to what may be unpleasant but nonetheless relevant, they might not recognise a problem, threat or opportunity when it arises.

The wrong information

Next, there are problems relating to the content of the information itself:

- Origin, reliability and accuracy
  - are the sources known and vetted?
- Cost
  - how reliable is it if it's free?
  - how can we justify expenditure if it's expensive?
- Comprehensiveness
  - how do I know if I have all I need, or if critical elements are missing?
- Selectivity
  - marvellous not to be flooded with hundreds of pages, but what are the grounds for selection, or omission?

In the real world of course, it is impossible to have 100% certainty, and decisions have to be taken on imperfect information because of all sorts of pressures, usually time and money. Nonetheless, it is not impossible to establish practical checklists which we can apply rapidly in cases of need.

Checklist: right or wrong information
- Where does this come from? Did I ask for it?
- Should I file it, store it, bin it, or pass it on?
- Do I need it now?
- Is it worth keeping for future use?
- Is it worth passing to someone else? How do I know?
- Could I get hold of it again easily if the need arises?
- Would I know where to go for it?
- Does it need a lot of work on it or is it usable now?
- If it hadn't arrived, would or should I have gone looking for it?

Computers

Millions have been spent on integrated information systems to provide direct links between, for example, production, accounts, sales and marketing, using the best modern technology available. It has now been demonstrated, however, that implementing sophisticated information systems can cause more problems than it solves.

Many managers do not rely on computer-based information to make decisions. For those who have no option but to do so, there are as many again who get most of their information from face-to-face or telephone conversations. The rest comes from documents which come from outside the organisation, such as journals or reports.

There have been numerous studies which have attempted to prove the competitive advantage of IT systems and there has been an overwhelming body of literature reporting that IT has not repaid its investment. At last we are beginning to understand why.

Information systems

At the risk of oversimplification, it is arguable that in implementing IT systems, an organisation will hit some obstacles, the reasons for which will include the following:

- Those developing the systems have oversimplified, and possibly, wrong ideas of what is to be accomplished
- The approach is one of getting the users to fit the system adopted, not, as it should be, the other way round
- Purchasing decisions are made by those who won't be using the technology themselves, or by those who don't know accurately the jobs of those who will

- The systems are designed with lack of, or minimal reference to, those who do the jobs
- The systems designers don't take into account the way their systems will change the organisation structure and take little account of proper learning and training
- The systems designers take no account of the social values of the organisation i.e. the way people work

People

The success of the system will depend on the level of participation of all the relevant people who work in it. The process of change has to meet the needs of the activities they perform, and therefore their needs too. The system must take account of the need of people to cooperate effectively. People responsible for specific tasks should contribute to defining how those tasks should be done and how they should be combined into jobs and systems activities. The system should also take into account the following:

- Managers still prefer to get information from people
- Managers prefer to add value by interpretation
- People don't share information easily
- The more complex a system, the less likely it is to change people's working behaviour, especially if they have had little or no input to building it
- The use people make of an IT system is proportional to the participation they have had in specifying it
- People who don't communicate face to face will not find it easier to communicate through computers

The key is to involve people throughout and gain a full understanding of the culture of the organisation.

Organisational culture

An inhibitor to information users – as opposed to planners or 'systems' people – taking an active part in the construction of the system may be the culture of the organisation itself. The following stereotypes may help you to identify your own position:

Organisation A
- Ideas come from individuals
- People are responsible and motivated
- Action is reached by discussion and debate
- Open debate and discussion are normal
- Informal atmosphere and few closed doors

Organisation B
- Acceptable ideas come from senior people
- People are capable of loyalty
- Action results from issuing instructions
- Each person has a strictly defined role
- An atmosphere of formality, a hush in the air, and deference to rank and agenda

Successful information management may flourish in either organisation, but the degree of structure and level of regimentation can be crucial, or lethal, to information sharing and creativity. If managing information is all about the free exchange of ideas between people in a changing environment, then we must plump for Organisation A. On the other hand, Organisation B's people should have a clear understanding of their roles and duties even if there is a 'hush in the air'. If cultural differences exist between different departments of the same organisation, it is doubtful whether those differences can be overcome by the imposition of new technology. In fact, it would probably make it worse.

With a people-centered approach, the organisation, or department, needs to carry out an audit of information activities.

The audit

No audit can be effective without taking account of the organisation's style of managing, its culture and its organisational structure. But the starting point is the organisation's objectives and priorities; it is only in relation to these that information flow, or lack of it, can have any significance.

The audit: basic questions
- What information is needed to support aims and objectives?
- What information is available?
- How is it used?
- What are the differences between what is needed and what is available?
- What needs to be done to match needs with provision?
- How is information best delivered to its users?

Having established a general framework for action, the next stage is to get down to the detail of the information audit.

The information audit
1. What information do staff acquire? Where from? How is it used?
2. What information do staff create?
3. What do they do with it? Dump? Rewrite? Regenerate? Store?
4. What do they store it for? Do they do anything to it apart from filing? What purpose will it serve?
5. What do they send on or deliver? To whom? In what form?
6. Who are involved in these activities? What are their responsibilities?
7. What equipment do they have? Hardware, software, filing cabinets etc.?
8. Are there any control documents? Policy statements? Guidelines? Procedures? Manuals?
9. Is any of the information redundant? Are any of the activities non-productive? Are results visible?
10. What budget is available? Who controls it?

Having identified the information activities and supporting resources, next is the question of assessing their effectiveness:

- To what extent does this activity or resource support objectives and priorities?
- How efficient is it in terms of the time and money required to do it?
- Is it adaptable to fit changing needs?
- Are any direct results or benefits visible?

The audit requires an inventory of the way people and technology mix to ensure that appropriate information gets to the people who need it. It also requires measures to evaluate the costs and benefits of the exercise. Once this has been mapped out, we should see where there is a good – and a bad – fit between what resources there are and what results they produce. It should show where information needs to be communicated between different functions but isn't currently. It should show where information is currently gathered and processed, but not required. It should also show gaping holes where results are not forthcoming because nobody is working on the information process.

Information costing and value

Value is often attributed by cost alone, for example, the cost of a database search, or the time taken to compile a report. This cost–value ratio may be influenced by the fact that information is not always regarded as the most valuable resource.

The problem with assigning a monetary value alone often means converting something qualitative, perhaps intangible, into a numeric figure. The real value of information may be also assessed otherwise, in more interpretative, qualitative terms. As we have seen, there are a number of other factors to consider whose value is more difficult to evaluate.

Information values
- Timeliness and appropriateness to the task
- Degree of accuracy, relevance and comprehensiveness
- Ease of access and use
- Impact on and contribution to decision-making
- Impact on efficiency and time-saving
- Contribution to meeting targets and new directions
- Contribution to cost-savings or profits

It is difficult to assign monetary values to all but the last of these measures. Whereas cost is obviously the key factor, all too often it is the only factor. Sometimes it may be necessary to weigh cost against time of access and delivery, or against potential impact or contribution. Sometimes these other values may override the restriction of a budget limit.

The same kind of judgements will need to be applied when we start searching tomorrow.

Summary

Today, we looked at planning and organising information to prevent things going wrong and to take account of the way people work and behave.

Checkpoint: Does the information system in my organisation create difficulties or inhibit the use of the information I need?

To help assess this, use the following checklist:

Checklist
1   Are information needs structured or are they considered only when they arise?
2   Does anyone know who needs what, apart from the individuals themselves?
3   Do you review your information sources?
4   Do you make do with what you have already?
5   Do you add value to the information you process?
6   Do you have a say in the hardware or software you use?
7   Do you make a contribution to how the job is done?
8   Do you get information in the right form? At the right time?
9   Is it reliable and accurate?
10 When you pass it on, do you know what will happen to it?

Searching and evaluating

When information hits the desk, we either act on it, store it, deliver it to someone else, or dump it. However, we are rather lucky if all the information we need just happens to arrive on its own. Much of it we have to look for; then we need to evaluate it. Today we will look at the different aspects involved in these two processes.

Searching and evaluating
- Different types of information
- Major search areas
- Desk-research techniques
- Evaluating information

The different types of information

The way in which information arrives affects the ease with which it can be manipulated and the speed with which it can be delivered for action. Conversion from one form to another is more often possible than not, but can take time which is not always planned for in rapid decision-making.

Many types of documents are increasingly in electronic form. In fact, most information probably starts that way, whether it be:

- Ad-hoc factual records such as memos, reports or diary entries
- Explanatory information contained in dictionaries, manuals, directories, handbooks or encyclopaedias
- References and pointers such as catalogues, brochures, abstracting and indexing services
- Text found in books, journals, newspapers, surveys, studies and reports
- Statistics on an international, national, organisational or local scale
- Time series in the form of production and sales figures, market trends, economic indices and financial data

Much of this will start its life being keyed or scanned in to a computer and much will continue in the form of a database, either for an organisation's use or for commercial access on-line or on CD-ROM, or, in many cases, both.

The major search areas

For an organisation, there are three basic origins of information

- Internal sources
- External sources
- Research

There is a fourth – happenstance – which is wonderful when it happens, but finding information by chance does not provide an adequate method on which we can rely.

Internal sources
Habit and ready availability lead us to look initially to the organisation's processes for what we need to know. By doing so, the limitations of what we find may exclude new information on any of the myriad factors which cause change: data on the economy, the changing market, legislation, the environment, new methods, skills and techniques, case-studies of other organisations. The experience of others, and intelligence on the world outside the organisation's four walls are now recognised as vital to competition and survival.

As information appears to be self-generating, even the internal routes become foggy, especially in larger organisations, and require guidance.

Information routers
- Information maps
- Audit trails
- Gatekeepers
- Groupware

Information maps   Despite the growth of internal company databases, few people know where to find what they are looking for inside the organisation. An information map, which describes where the most widely dispersed information can be found, is a simple enough device, but still a rarity. Pointers and guides to information on a shelf are easy enough to set up, but more valuable are pointers to the people who own or control particular kinds of information. Such an aid could be achieved by adding descriptors to the internal telephone directory, where job labels may not only confuse, but act as deterrents to information sharing.

Audit trails　A little more detailed and down to earth but practical for locating documents which are not where they should be. An audit trail enables traceability to the start or end of a process, identifying all the activities, people involved and locations along the way.

Gatekeepers　Before information was recognised as a resource to be managed like money, people and equipment, the 'gatekeeper' performed an unofficial role of pointing people in the right direction. The 'human guide' can be more important than paper or electronic pointers if there is a general unawareness of internal information resources. The gatekeeper may not only point people to the best sources, but help with information searches and reduce the time it takes for employees to find the right information.

Groupware   Groupware is a technology which enables different individuals to:

- Share documents electronically
- Help people work in teams across geographical or functional boundaries
- Discuss issues on-line
- Communicate and collaborate more efficiently
- Capture and disseminate key information easily for decision-making

DEC's *Teamlinks*, NCR's *Cooperation* and Lotus *Notes* are examples of Groupware, a technology whose success hinges as much on the culture and structure of the organisation as on the right hardware. Rigid and secretive information cultures and multilayered hierarchies tend to 'filter' information and slow progress to decisions. The purpose of Groupware is to get information direct from and to those who need it. Unless this is managed with the user in mind, it may well end up as yet more unexploited information technology. Training and human support are essential.

External sources
It is probably the climate of continuous change and competition which has made organisations look to the outside world and use information from it not just for competitive advantage, but often for survival. It is probably to databases, either on-line or on CD-ROM that more are turning for up-to-date information of all kinds. We will look both at databases and at their forerunners – libraries.

On-line databases   Most of the world's published output may be identified, located and retrieved to a pc via modem and using appropriate passwords. There are more than 7 000 commercial on-line databases available through the telephone lines or the national and international data networks, such as BT's *Global Network Services*. They cover every area of published research and activity and should form one of the first ports of call when embarking on a new project, or when trying to establish reliable information of any kind.

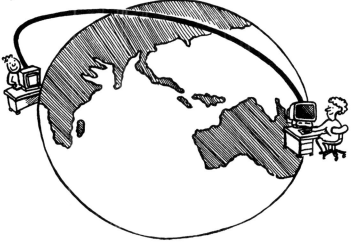

On-line databases are usually made available through agency or 'host' organisations. Two such major hosts which hold many of the databases referred to on Sunday are: **Datastar-Dialog** which holds hundreds of international databases covering all aspects of business, science, technology, the humanities and news services; **FT Profile** which holds the full text of many newspapers and reports from market research agencies and stockbrokers.

Guidance on how to tackle these, at least in the beginning, is advisable. To help with the identification of databases, there are directories and guides, even a database of databases is available on Datastar-Dialog. Some of the major ones are listed at the end of today.

CD-ROM databases   The rapid growth of CD-ROM (Compact Disk – Read Only Memory) technology enables the benefits of many of these databases to be available on your own pc without the need for a modem or connection to an external source. A CD-ROM can carry enormous amounts of data – 500 megabytes, or 300 000 A4 pages – and uses simple search software to enable rapid retrieval. New generations of search software based on menus or pull-down screens really are user friendly and require little or no training in their use.

Unlike on-line connections, you buy a CD-ROM database on subscription and run it in-house on a CD-ROM drive attached to your pc.

An apparatus known as a CD-ROM tower, or 'jukebox', enables simultaneous searching across a number of CD-ROMs. Networking systems, such as Novell, enable working from a number of linked pcs.

Libraries   Libraries full of information have been written on why people don't use libraries. There are a number of reasons proposed for this: a dowdy image and an unfriendly atmosphere among them. Mostly however, people simply don't know what is in them and suspect that they can't deliver what they want anyway. Many public libraries throughout the UK now offer access to on-line databases. Below is a brief list of professional organisations which have geared their resources to information services for the practising manager.

- Institute of Management
- Institute of Personnel and Development
- Chartered Institute of Marketing
- Chartered Institute of Bankers
- Institute of Directors
- Industrial Society
- Chartered Institute of Management Accountants

These organisations offer services primarily to members, but, in certain cases, to non-members as well, on a fee-paying basis.

Many business-school libraries offer information services to organisations on a brokerage basis.

Desk research

For research to be successful, it will need to pull diverse information sources together, and adapt and collate findings for delivery systematically. There are a number of ways of tackling this and techniques of investigation and information analysis include:

- Gathering all sources of relevant information and proceeding by logical deduction; a question of being clear on how information fits needs, extracting the significant from the mass, and cutting out or rejecting the dross
- A detailed approach which tests and retests, and provides a scientific conclusion supported by the evidence
- Familiarisation and regular contact with the area of research; a question of rooting out the experts and listening to others
- Action research: putting hypotheses to the test; try it out, and see how it works

The ideal research method would entail:

- Adopting a systematic approach to collecting information
- Paying attention to detail
- Applying logical reasoning
- Listening to those with a contribution to make
- Consistent questioning and probing
- Gaining an intuitive feel for the problem by steady familiarisation with it

A simplified research approach would entail:

1 Establishing who the users are
2 Identifying the important questions
3 Obtaining information from internal sources
4 Obtaining information from external sources
5 Culling, analysing, compiling and reporting

Our research techniques can also help us with criteria to evaluate information.

Evaluation

Having researched your information, the final thing to do before you act on it, store it, deliver it or reject it, is to put it to some kind of test. This can be a fairly rapid or quite lengthy process.

It may be immediately obvious that the information you have is highly relevant, or you may have to submit it to further evaluation. The key to evaluation is the objectives or targets to which you are working. This presupposes a working knowledge of the information users (decision-makers, problem-solvers), and at least a notion of the use they have in mind. This may appear obvious, but all too often this does not happen. To be able to separate the wheat from the chaff, we must ask questions on behalf of the information users and then sift the information to provide answers. The alternative is to find answers to questions that have not been asked.

Even this can be too much of a black and white approach.
Models and guidelines are no respecter of poor briefings,
impossible deadlines and demanding bosses. When time is
pressing, something imperfect is probably better than
nothing. If time is available then precision and conciseness
become more important. Overall, it is useful to keep four
key elements in mind:

1	Objectives	What?
2	Users	Who?
3	Time frame	When?
4	Purpose	Why?

There is a fifth: Format – How?, which relates to adding
value and manipulating data for delivery with which we
deal on Friday.

In determining whether information is relevant or not, it is
useful to remember that it is a resource to be exploited, or
wasted, like any other; relevance equals time saving and
information overload equals non-information. The following
checklist can provide a starting point.

- Does this help contribute towards my objectives?
- Might this be useful to someone else?
- Am I passing the buck?
- If I dump it, what is lost?
- Would I know where to get it back if needed?
- Is the information practical, or theory-based?
- Is it speculative, or substantiated?
- If controversial, is it supported by evidence?
- Is it selective, or comprehensive?
- Is it directly about the subject in question?

Summary

When using information we have to be certain of its value.
Today, we have studied where to look for the relevant
information and, even more importantly, how to evaluate it.

Checkpoint: If satisfying my information needs is delegated
to someone else, am I and are they clear on exactly what I
need?

Tomorrow, we will look at effective storage and retrieval of
information.

Sources of information

Gale Directory of Databases Gale Research International.

On-line/CD-ROM Business Sourcebook Pam Foster (ed.),
Headland Press.

The CD-ROM Directory TFPL Publishing.

ASLIB, The Association for Information Management,
20 – 24 Old St, London EC1V. Tel. 0171 253 4488

Datastar-Dialog Europe, Haymarket House, 28 Haymarket,
London SW1Y 4ER. Tel. 0171 930 7646

FT Profile, PO Box 12, Sunbury on Thames, Middlesex
TW16 7UD. Tel. 01932 761444

Storing information

Today, we will look at the different factors involved in storing information:

- Collection and supply vs. supply on demand
- Ways of storing documents
- Filing systems
- Databases

The first thing to establish is whether you need information readily available or not; if you don't, don't store it!

Collection and supply vs. supply on demand

That which you buy to keep for future use should become an asset. The danger is that too much information becomes an overhead along with the costs of space and time taken to process it.

The most efficient way to keep overheads down and value up is to strike a balance between the core items you need available regularly, and access to the rest by phone, fax, computer link or personal contact.

Remember that information is the one resource that consumes all the others of time, people, finance, equipment and space. The choice is therefore between collection for ready availability, with its incumbent costs, and supply on demand, with its requisite knowledge of where and how to obtain information in the time available.

The following questions should help:

* Will I need this?
* Will it be expensive to buy and keep?
* Can I get hold of it easily if the need arises?
* Would I know how to get access to it?
* Does the benefit of processing and storage truly outweigh the difficulty of obtaining it on demand?

If the answer to the last question is yes, then we must decide on the best method of storage.

For storing documents we need both a method of containing them and a filing system to retrieve them easily. For storing many kinds of records, the database is now the most appropriate method. We will now look at each of these elements in turn.

Document storage

Paper
It has been said that the other people (apart from computer manufacturers) to make a fortune out of the age of

computerisation and the 'paperless' office are those who manufacture filing cabinets. The more we computerise, the more hard copy we produce and thus the more paper records we seem to need to keep.

Although many of us prefer to see information and results on paper, this is now slowly changing. Storage of documents on paper is increasingly expensive, not only because of the space it consumes and the time needed to organise it, but also because of the raw material cost itself.

Microform
Although the age of microform seems to have passed, it may still present an efficient alternative to paper for storing large amounts of internally created documents which are needed for legal or support purposes. Conversion from paper to microfilm or microfiche and vice-versa is now a well practised technology. A link to a computer can accelerate the retrieval of a specific document, although reading microform documents on perspex screens can be an inhibitor to long-term or everyday use.

Magnetic tape or disk

This has become a standard means of document storage although digital audio tape (DAT) is beginning to offer greater storage capacity and lower costs than magnetic tape. As central processors switch over to networked pcs, high-density storage and information transfer on $3\frac{1}{2}$ inch disks increasingly make the electronic option more attractive than microform.

CD-ROM

The CD-ROM has become an attractive storage option because of its size, its durability and the speed and ease which it offers for document retrieval. The cost of 'pressing' data on to CD-ROM is continually dropping; it will not be long before it becomes a 'back-garden' or 'garage' operation.

Filing systems

Often considered the most humdrum and menial of activities, efficient filing systems are at the centre of operations of any successful organisation.

Humdrum or not, we have all been stymied by 'personal' filing systems which defy consistency, logic, and finding the document in question! Whether the system is manual or computerised, it is essential to have a standard method for describing information. Describing information is called indexing and there are a number of approaches to it.

Indexing

One of the most common practices is to index and file under personal or organisation name. For consistency and to save time it is advisable to decide whether to file, for example, under:

- Van Gogh, or Gogh, van or Vincent
- IM or Institute of Management
- Department of Trade and Industry, or Trade and Industry, Department of, or DTI

Names are a principal descriptor but they do not cater for the wide range of subjects under which we may need to store documents. We are fortunate if we know the exact name or title of the document we need. More often than not, information searching is characterised by vagueness and expressed in terms of subjects.

Word indexing
Computer databases enable word indexing, a simple method of describing the document by reference to individual words or phrases which occur in the text. This is often called free-text indexing where every word can become an index term for the document in which it occurs.

The free-text method is not always as specific for retrieving documents as may be required, especially when using terms which may have different meanings depending on the context.

For example, the training function may well need to collect information on competences, NVQs, outward bound, T-groups, self-study etc. all of which may refer to learning methods. Unless this is categorised with some detail and accuracy, training personnel could find themselves looking through everything each time they need a specific subject. For this reason, it may be more appropriate to adopt some form of subject indexing.

Subject indexing
Subject indexing involves analysing the subject matter of a document and choosing appropriate terms to represent it. As we have seen, the effectiveness of this depends on using terminology with consistency; hence you will need an index which helps you select the right term. This can be a thesaurus of terms which shows the relationships of one term to another, so that you know whether to use, for example, 'computers' or 'automation' or 'new technology' or 'information technology' to describe accurately the document's content. Consistency is again the key. Using a ready-made index or thesaurus could save hours of reinventing the wheel.

Databases

Card indexes, diaries, Filofaxes and personal organisers are devices which hold databases, usually of events, contacts, dates, agendas, ideas or other such personal data. However, for the mass of working information on, for example, customers, competitors, or personnel and training records, these kinds of devices are not adequate. Nor are they designed to be. For recording, sifting and sorting different data on different subjects you need a computer with database software.

As we have seen earlier in the week, there are thousands of databases covering all sectors of commercial, business, scientific and technical information which are available on-line or on CD-ROM. Following our policy of not doing what others have done already therefore, why set up a database?

Why set up a database?
A telephone directory is an example of a large scale manual database. The differences between it and a computerised database are:

- That it is only for one user at a time – if you need access for 10 users at the same time, you need to buy 10 copies
- It only has one point of entry – you can only look up one thing at one place at one time
- It is not reusable – you cannot amend, edit or modify it without for example rekeying it or scanning it into a computer (and you cannot even do that unless you have permission, as we shall see on Saturday)

Computerised databases have a number of advantages:

- They are suitable for many simultaneous users
- Electronic information is reusable
- There can be many points of access to a document
- They enable information to be supplied on demand
- They enable easy information transfer to another computer by downloading (making a copy) or disk copying

There are, however, as many bad reasons as there are good ones for setting up a database:

Bad reasons
- To save money (it doesn't work)
- To exploit hardware (as opposed to what people need)
- 'Everybody else is doing it' (perhaps they shouldn't)
- Empowering users to share information (imposing IT systems does not mean that they will)

Good reasons
- To sort, manipulate and retrieve information faster
- To produce information more flexibly and efficiently
- To store information more easily and usefully
- To provide access to many people at the same time
- To provide customers with a better service
- To enable people to do their jobs more effectively

Setting up a database: first decisions
We will need to establish some basic requirements:

- Who wants what out of the database? Lists, labels, literature, references, reports?
- Who is the database for and who is going to search it? Staff, customers, the public, a select few?
- What is to go into the database? The most used, most labour-intensive, most changeable paperwork?
- Who uses what now?
- Who needs what now and does not have it?
- How is the data to be handled or collected?
- Is it to be searchable by codes, keywords or free-text?
- Is it for storing information indefinitely or will the information be dumped after a certain time?
- Is there a database already in existence which, partially or wholly, meets the requirements?

How the information comes out will depend largely on how it goes in. Hence it is vital to know what the database must achieve, or, in other words, what the expectations are of it. We must also ask if it is to store references or complete

records. This last question is vital as much for reasons of ownership and legality (see Saturday) as for avoidance of confusion. It is key to the provision of a consistent structure which traditional database systems require for effective retrieval. For example, a customer database will have different objectives, contents, purposes and structure from a competitor database. Different structures will have different formats.

Examples of database record formats

Customers	**Competitors**	**Training records**
Name, address	Name, address	Name, department
Postcode	Product(s)	Current/past post
Product	Market share	Qualifications
Purchase date	Image	Courses
Payment	Share price	Initiatives
Problems	Growth	Projects
Servicing	Debt/reserves	Experience
Complaints	Gross income	Promotions

Most database management software should permit the construction of different records to fit different needs. Some can retrieve the information quicker than others. Some can mix and match from different files to create new information.

The greatest advantage of 'text retrieval packages' is that they can pinpoint and retrieve a specific word from masses of text very rapidly. However, they are not so effective in the integration of data from a number of separate files, for example, drawing off data from both a customer database and training database to create a synthesis of information may prove difficult. For this a 'Relational database system' which enables different databases to 'interrelate', or 'speak' to each other would be more appropriate.

Once we have made the decisions on the need for and nature of the database, then we need to identify which particular package is most suitable to accommodate those needs. To consult one or two directories such as listed below is a practical starting point. Once we have one or two ideas on a particular package, it is useful to contact those organisations already using it. They should know it, warts and all, and may save us much pain. If there aren't any others already using it, then we are in trouble, because it means that we are pioneering the product. Pioneering can be a real headache and may prove expensive.

Summary

Today, we have looked at the most effective ways of storing information in order to be certain of its easy retrieval.

Checkpoint: Have I identified a couple of specific sources which I need regularly?

Tomorrow, we will examine the delivery of information and its use in reports and presentations.

Sources of information

European Directory of Text Retrieval Systems Gower.

Software Users Year Book VNU Business Publications.

Delivering information

So far we have identified that we have an information need. We have searched for it using either internal or external sources, or both. We have evaluated it and decided to bin it, store it, or put it to use.

Towards the end of the information life cycle, that use involves delivering it, usually in one of the following ways:

- Electronic transfer
- Writing a report
- Giving a presentation

Electronic transfer

This is the most direct form of information delivery and increasingly the most cost-effective. Although terms such as data transfer, electronic data interchange, wide-area networks and the Internet are all a source of confusion at the outset, often they are revealed as no more than jargon for fairly straightforward operations once we understand them.

There are a number of ways of delivering information, or electronically transferring it from one location or computer to another.

- Tape or disk
- Telecommunications transfer
- E-mail
- The Internet

Tape or disk
Tape or disk transfer provides a physical method of delivering information in the most flexible way; information remains easy to amend, edit, modify and integrate into other files. It involves copying files on to tape or disk, putting it into a jiffy bag and sending it to the recipient. Thankfully problems of compatibility, or using data created on one computer or another, have largely been overcome through standard data formats, such as ASCII (American Standard Code for Information Interchange), and the widespread use of common operating systems such as MSDOS and WINDOWS.

Half-inch magnetic tap is giving way to DAT (digital audio tape) as a transfer mechanism. DAT tapes are held on miniature cassettes and hold larger amounts of data than magnetic tape, and the tape drives are increasingly available as standard.

Telecommunications transfer

An equally simple and direct method of getting data from computer A to computer B is to send it through a network line. This can be a physical cable which requires a capital investment and therefore an assessment of predicted use. The cable link requires two like computers at either end, or software which enables them to be compatible, 'interface', or 'talk to each other.'

We would normally find physical cabling used within an organisation on a LAN (local area network). If a cable is too expensive to install for communications outside the organisation on a WAN (wide area network), the next method to explore is via the telephone lines or data networks.

The data networks, as represented principally in the UK by BT's *Global Network Services* (GNS), can be fast, cheap and now offer error correction, or the delivery of data from one computer to another free of interference or corruption. Many countries have now established their own data networks and these are linked together providing an international network. The UK's GNS can link direct to *Transpac* in France, *Eirpac* in Ireland or *Hellaspac* in Greece to name but a few.

Both telephone and data lines require our computer to have a modem and also preferably communications software to ease connections, send and receive the data and emulate the computer at the other end if it's not the same. The question of compatibility or interfacing is no IT trick, or manufacturer's con. Our car requires special parts which will not fit any other, just as a Zanussi washing machine will not be too happy fitted with Indesit parts. Likewise, through a telecommunications link, a computer will need to know to whom it is talking.

E(lectronic)-mail

E-mail enables the transmission and receipt of messages and documents using computers and telecommunications' lines as letter-boxes and postal services. The 'letter' is sent to and sits in a mail-box on the recipient's computer until it is disposed of. E-mail is available not only on local internal systems but also through national commercial systems to remote locations via the telecommunications networks. For remote E-mail, users need a contract with a supplier, such as BT, which will supply them with an E-mail address – a highly specific, yet still somewhat cumbersome code.

E-mail has its advantages over the telephone and letter-writing. It is faster and cheaper than ordinary mail and does not require the recipient to be present. E-mail also enables one message or document to be 'mailed' to any number of recipients. Its disadvantages, as usual with IT, only arise from misuse or abuse. Like any tools, communication tools need to be handled properly.

The Internet

The Internet is basically the world's largest network of E-mail users. There are now millions of subscribers to it and new subscriptions are at the rate of hundreds per week. But it is more than a worldwide E-mail network. It enables access to thousands of sources of information as well, such as the on-line databases we mentioned on Sunday and Tuesday, library catalogues, bulletin boards, specialist discussion groups, even 'virtual' shopping. With the Internet, so it is claimed, the global village is finally here.

Finding your way round the Internet, or 'navigating the net', can be a time-consuming problem, although software such as *Mosaic* (in Internet terms known as a 'browser') is making the journey easier. You need to find the cheapest phone route into the system. It may be cheaper, for example, to use Mercury to make a long-distance phone call direct to an Internet node, than use BT for a local call. You also need a fast modem, as slower ones will keep you waiting and push up telephone bills.

While the Internet is an unprecedented means of both *seeking* and *delivering* information, it has its own unwritten code of manners: it has its own jargon or 'netspeak'; frowns heavily on brash advertising; and seems, at least for the moment, to be resisting attempts to become commercial. Payment 'on-line' is a current difficulty although much of the information on the Internet is free of charge. This situation is in a process of rapid change and development and is worth monitoring and exploring.

In the UK, academic bodies are signed up to the Internet via a network called JANET (joint academic network). Others can sign up via commercial agents such as DEMON, CIX, PIPEX or COMPuSERVE (an on-line network which has been established for some years). Prices vary. Dial-up-access to many Internet features can total about £10 per month. Sending E-mail, reading reports and searching some databases can come to £7 – £10 per week. Caution is advisable as 'on-line' time can mount up, and some services charge more than others.

On the other hand, the Internet can provide contacts and information on a scale hitherto unimaginable by putting out a query to a bulletin board or discussion group and getting replies from all over the world.

On the other hand, it can deliver a lot of clutter and junk mail not too dissimilar to that which comes through your letter-box. At the time of writing, the Internet needs the investment of a considerable amount of time to get to know it and derive the most benefits from it. But it is here to stay and growing very fast.

Writing a report

More often than not, it will be necessary to work on the information we have gathered, selected and evaluated before we deliver it. Whatever means we choose to get it to the end-user, we will probably need to write it into a shape fit for its recipient(s). The final outcome of this will usually be a report.

Report-writing seems relatively straightforward until we get down to it. Then we find how easy it is to become unstuck. Guidelines on report-writing best practice can be summarised as follows:

1 Make sure the aims and objectives are clear, and construct a clear introduction
2 Provide a summary of major findings, recommendations and action points, preferably on one page
3 Establish the best order from the reader's viewpoint
4 Work out a clear, logical structure and don't wait for inspiration to strike for the first draft
5 Divide the main body into headed sections and use diagrams and charts for clarity
6 Use the simplest language possible, avoiding long words, technical jargon and especially long sentences; take care over spelling, punctuation and repetition. It would be a shame to be floored by a technical foul
7 Make use of indenting, bold, and different typeface etc. for the key concepts you wish to highlight
8 Keep it focused, make it concise and don't waffle

9 Make sure in advance that proposals will not cause nasty shocks, by discussing drafts with colleagues or superiors, but do not shirk major issues which the information supports

10 Pay attention to the final presentation. To overcook a simple report with gold-embossed binding is as inappropriate as handing in a final document in long-hand

An alternative to printing a report and circulating it for discussion: send it via E-mail to your discussion group for comments thus ensuring a saving of time, travel and paper!

Presentations

The final report may well need to be presented orally to a number of people. If this is the case, it is probably advisable to circulate copies, or summaries, to the audience in advance. Although this is good practice, it is also sensible to assume that the recipients will not have digested its contents in the knowledge that an explanatory presentation is to come.

We will concentrate on the information content of presentations with emphasis on graphics and charts, because, as the saying goes, a picture can paint a thousand words.

Graphics and charts

If it supports or clarifies your case, use graphical representation for what you have to say. It is not only more eye-catching, it can also make your point more effectively than the written word or statistic. Such would be the case for example for an overview of current expenditures, expected returns on investment, improvements or deteriorations in future sales, a relationship between advertising spend and sales figures, competitors' performance, or a description of potential market segments.

There are a number of options for deriving graphic illustrations from statistics. Graphics packages may well come with the purchase of standard hardware package. Many spreadsheets and word-processing packages are now equipped with graphics capability. Some of the options for presentation purposes include:

- Flow charts give a visual description of how a process works or how work flows from one area to another. They can show the when, where and how of activities and of contributions

- Histograms, pie charts and bar charts take a snapshot of our process and show how it is performing. They are useful for showing the impact of one factor against another, such as income over time, or complaints or faults of a particular process, or customer calls against sales
- Fishbone diagrams attempt to relate causes and effects. They combine the creative process of brainstorming with the organisation of a decision-tree in trying to examine all related and unrelated possibilities of a certain process going wrong.
- Scatter diagrams plot the occurrence of failure, for example, hold-ups in production against failure to meet customer delivery over time, or the use of one supplier against hold-ups in production. They enable confirmation or denial of suspected relationships

Graphics and charts

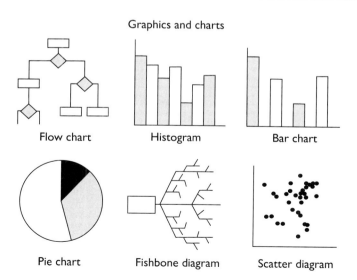

Flow chart   Histogram   Bar chart

Pie chart   Fishbone diagram   Scatter diagram

Having decided which illustrations to use, if any, let us next work on transposing our report into a presentation:

1 Keep it short. Fifteen minutes is a long time to listen
2 Don't try to impress for the sake of it, and don't clutter with too much detail
3 Concentrate on attracting attention and holding interest by making the message understandable and memorable
4 Choose a presentation structure and stick to it:
  – an account which is logical may well be boring
  – people like stories, but they have to be good
  – a model such as what, why, how, when, where, who offers a safer bet

The key to success is in the preparation of the information to be delivered. A main, arresting point may be a better starter than the usual joke, even something controversial if appropriate and/or if the information supports it. The main body of the presentation should be smooth, simple and authoritative, allowing the information to make its mark.

The closing remarks should focus on the main findings, and suggest challenges or next steps, make recommendations, call to action, raise questions or call for answers. The objective, as with a report, is to present a course of action, or lead to a decision which will produce the benefits presented.

Summary

Today, we have looked at electronic delivery of information and the essential elements in report-writing and presentation.

Checkpoint: Do I do enough to tailor the information I process to the needs of its recipients?

Tomorrow, we will examine the role and use of information in the process of decision-making and problem-solving.

Sources of information

Demon	Tel. 0181 349 0063
CIX	Tel. 0181 390 8446
PIPEX	Tel. 01223 250120
COMPuSERVE	Tel. 0800 289458
BT Mailbox	Tel. 0800 800 916

Information in problem-solving and decision-making

If information does not lead to some kind of action then arguably it will have little or no value. It has often been said that there is a relationship between information and decision-making but it is hard to prove, often enough because a decision may be made for many diverse reasons and causes.

So how do we put information to use to help make decisions and solve problems?

Today we will look at the following:

Using information
- In workshops
- For problem-solving
- For decision-making

Workshops

Workshops are vehicles for brainstorming sessions, and for moving from 'Where are we now?' to 'Where do we want to be?'

Workshops are principally gatherings of anything from four to 14 people called together to tackle a problem or achieve an objective. They are suitable for putting people in a relaxed and creative environment in order to tackle a particular issue where information needs to be sought, agreed, shared and owned by the participants, where a deadlock needs to be resolved, or a decision made. The workshop does not so much rely on an expert contributor to deliver information as on a good facilitator to handle it and the people involved. Workshops focus on participation and involvement rather than just listening or watching and they can generate ownership of the issue in question.

Good workshops practice is as much about effective people management as it is about information handling. For a successful workshop we need a good facilitator who will ensure a number of key practices:

- Only those with a contribution should attend
- An atmosphere conducive to free discussion
- Encouragement of participation
- Careful handling of red herrings
- Focus on the objectives
- That the right questions are raised
- That appropriate comments are pulled together
- That follow-up action is clarified

Defining problem-solving and decision-making

In a working environment of rapid change and reaction, problem-solving and decision-making are amongst the most highly valued of management skills and the most important uses to which information is applied. Although the techniques appear similar and in many cases need to be interchangeable, they are quite different. Consider the following statements:

- My computer won't work
- The number of complaints has risen
- Our suppliers aren't delivering to time any more
- Staff turnover on the factory floor has doubled
- Sales are down
- Staff morale is rock bottom

and these:

- Which new car shall I buy?
- Where shall we go on holiday?
- Shall we introduce a new performance appraisal scheme?
- Which of the candidates shall we appoint?
- Which road shall we take here?
- If we reorganise, what will be the impact on staff?

In the first set of statements, something has gone wrong; something is not behaving as it should. A deviation from the norm means we have to find out what went wrong in order to put it right. Problem-solving means finding the cause.

In the second set of statements, there is nothing wrong, rather a choice between a different set of alternatives. Indeed, some of the second set could well incorporate problems to solve along the way but the principal activity is one of finding the right choice.

One of the most frequent actions is to guess the cause of a problem and jump straight to a decision without knowing if the problem has been solved in the first place. For example:

- Spending more money on marketing without knowing why sales have dropped
- Changing suppliers without knowing why deliveries have slowed
- Stepping up quality control without analysing the nature of the complaints
- Having a staff party without knowing why morale is low

Information is central to both problem-solving and decision-making. Equally it can be said that failure to solve problems or take effective decisions is due to the lack of information.

Problem-solving

Let us take the problem of switching the light on and the room remaining in darkness. We would not go to any elaborate detail or information gathering exercise (except perhaps to find a torch, which is never where it should be!). Basically we know enough about this common occurrence to try one or two simple steps. It is common sense to try the most simple things first and then move on to the more complex.

However, if a problem of greater complexity arises then it is not so easy or advisable to try quick solutions. The cause of the problem may be in any one of a number of areas. A rising tide of complaints, for example, could stem from product deficiency, faulty machinery, poor delivery, unsafe packaging, incomplete documentation, publicity creating a false expectation, staff absence, unsatisfactory working conditions. The list is endless. We need to narrow the list down by analysing the complaints, checking out the information and getting the situation back to normal. This information gathering may be simple or complex but it is essential for discovering causes and solving problems.

The following stages should be followed in any systematic method of problem-solving:

1 Defining the problem
This involves an investigation to find out what exactly has gone wrong. Getting the definition right is vital, otherwise you will be solving the wrong problem and collecting answers to questions which have not been asked.

2 Gathering the information
This involves factors which may have an influence on the problem. It is worth doing this in some detail, discovering the people, activities, processes, time-scales and conditions under which the problem occurs.

3 Identifying causes
Causes usually relate to people, systems or equipment. Here again it is worth a good deal of checking to avoid jumping to the conclusion that it is the tool and not the operator, or vice versa. The question – what has changed from the norm? – often helps to identify where the cause is.

4 Identifying a possible solution
The testing stage is vital. You need to know how to choose the best alternative to try, to know exactly what you are looking for and how you will know if you are right.

This problem analysis approach was put forward some years ago by Kepner and Tregoe (*The New Rational Manager* John Martin, 1981) and the example opposite illustrates the stages of their method, which has proved effective in dealing with complex problems.

Decision-making

Effective decision-making practice, that is, selecting from alternatives, is also laid out by Kepner-Tregoe. It, too, has a heavy reliance on method and information, and involves a number of steps:

1 *Define the decision to be made*
This helps to clarify thinking, helps communication and provides a record for the future.

2 *Establish the objectives*
These are things that are desired from the decision and should be measurable where possible. This stage could involve a level of information searching and checking.

3 *Classify the objectives*
This is a case of differentiating those that must be achieved ('musts') from those that would be desirable but not essential to achieve ('wants'). The difference here is that if a 'must' is not achieved, then the option should be rejected.

4 *Musts*
To be valid a 'must', an objective should have a quantitative measure or an objective standard.

Problem analysis approach: example

1	What is the problem?	Staff morale
	What is not the problem?	Staff pay
	What is distinctive about the problem?	It's not wages
2	Where is the problem?	In production
	Where is not the problem?	Marketing, accounts, sales
	What is different about the problem?	Productivity
3	Who is affected by it?	Production workers?
	Who is not affected by it?	Distribution, sales
	What is different about those affected?	Absenteeism
4	To whom is the problem attached?	Production
	Who has not got the problem?	Anyone else
	What is different about them?	Contribution, productivity, increased absence
5	What things are affected by the problem?	Meeting deadlines, operational downturn, staff relations
	What things are not affected?	Machine capacity
	What is distinctive about those affected?	New air of discontent, rumblings
6	When and how often does it occur?	Mondays and Fridays
	When does it not occur?	Tues,Wed,Thurs
	What is different about the time it occurs?	Start of new work teams and schedules
7	When did the problem first occur?	5-6 weeks ago
	When did it not exist?	Before then
	What changed?	Introduction of new self-directed work teams
8	What changes might be relevant?	New work practices!
	What causes might this suggest?	Imposition of new scheme; lack of consultation; possible dominance of certain individuals?
	Test the possible causes	

5 *Wants*
The 'wants' should be examined for importance and given a numerical weighting, e.g. a score out of 10 for the most important, or less for something less important.

6 *Generate the alternatives*
It is at this stage that our information requirements have been established and the information seeking begins. Possible alternatives should be sought and listed.

7 *Applying the information*
Information should be obtained and recorded for each alternative against each 'must' objective.

8 *Testing alternatives against the 'musts'*
Those that do not meet the criteria established should be rejected.

9 *Scoring remaining alternatives against the 'wants'*
All alternatives should be compared and scored against each of the 'wants' in turn. The alternative that meets them best should be scored top and others allocated proportionate scores.

10 *Multiply the weights by the scores*
Add results up for each alternative to come to a provisional decision.

A provisional decision is reached by a process of elimination from the information gathered and scoring on the features which are desirable rather than essential. This can only offer a provisional decision, although rational, and even better, defensible. The example opposite shows the process in practice.

Effective decision-making

1	Decision definition	To buy a new computer
2	Establish the objectives	modem, expandable memory slot, 486 processor, max £1 000 price, CD-ROM drive, large hard disc, storage, Microsoft Works for Windows
3	Classify the objectives	Max. price Min. processor Max. hard disc storage Modem, CD-ROM drive, memory slot, MS Works for Windows
4	Musts	Max. price £1 000 Min. 486 processor Min. 200 megabyte hard disc
5	Wants	Fast modem: Score up to 10 Inbuilt CD-ROM: 10 Memory slot: 8 MS works for W: 6
6	Generate alternatives	Seek out information from suppliers, contacts, demos, reviews, reports etc.
7	Applying the information	Record information obtained against each 'must'
8	Testing against 'musts'	Do any of the alternatives not match against the musts e.g. on price, storage, or processor? Failure to match means rejection of the alternative
9	Scoring against 'wants'	Score remaining alternatives against the wants e.g. a slower modem would score 6/10, lack of a CD-ROM drive 0/10
10	Weight x scores	fast modem = 10 x 10 slow modem = 6 x 10 inbuilt CD-ROM = 10 x 10 No CD-ROM drive = 0 x 10
11	Add up the scores for a provisional decision	

This approach has been criticised as a method which may be too time consuming in fast-moving situations. However, its value is in its thoroughness and its requirement of systematic and pertinent information-gathering and not just the information leading to preconceived or politically acceptable conclusions.

It should be possible to see which are the best options and which are the not so good. The analysis will not provide an automatic decision. It may be important to re-examine the scores and weights and even the information on which they have been based. The method will, however, offer a sound framework for clear examination and provide evidence on how a decision was reached, especially in the case of complex or fuzzy choices.

Summary

Today, we have assessed the importance and value of information in the process of decision-making and problem-solving.

Checkpoint: Do I make decisions without sufficient information?

Tomorrow, we will study the various rules and regulations which govern the use of certain information.

Information and the law

Today, we look at some legal constraints which may prevent us from doing whatsoever we like with the information we have obtained. The law, as embodied in the Copyright, Designs and Patents Act (1988) and the Data Protection Act (1984), has an overriding impact on the way we handle information. Today we look at the affects these two laws have on our dealings with information.

- Copyright
- Data protection

Copyright

Copyright is concerned with preventing others from copying the copyright work. It is important to point out that copyright law can be very complex and may well require specialist legal advice. It has a far-reaching impact on the workplace as it can affect everything we use in the daily conduct of business, including advertising literature, terms

and conditions, journal or newspaper articles, computer programmes, drawings, plans, videos or databases.

Copyright can apply to anything created by anyone, be it a story, a photo, a painting or sculpture. Usually, unless the circumstances are exceptional, anything we create (report, design or system) for the organisation which employs us will be owned by that organisation, i.e. they own the copyright of that work and will want to protect it. In the case of a design, this protection may well be a patent. With documents it is a question of copyright. It is when and how we use the works of others, and others use ours, that copyright law comes into action to protect authors', publishers' and producers' rights against unlawful copying and to establish a framework of what we can and cannot do.

The following gives a brief outline of the rules for copying information for **internal use** in our organisation. We *cannot*, for example, without a licence or permission:

- Copy more than one article from one journal at the same time
- Copy multiple numbers of that article for distribution
- Store that copied document in our own in-house system
- Copy newspaper articles for distribution when they are no longer 'news' . . . i.e. new
- Copy more than one chapter, or 10%, of a book
- Store any document in a form (e.g. electronic or microform) other than that in which it was produced
- Copy, reproduce or pass on data from databases
- Run software on computers
- Copy video-cassettes

If we intend to publish, sell or distribute more widely the copied information, then we must seek permission from the copyright holder(s). This is best achieved by applying to the author and publisher. A fee may be payable, but this is certainly preferable to the possible penalties incurred where permission has not been obtained and this is discovered.

Copyright Licensing Agency (CLA)
This was set up before the 1988 Act to represent publishers in obtaining **a**) fair recompense for publishers and authors for the copying of their works, and **b**) granting licences to organisations for specified amounts of copying.

Such a licence to an organisation may be based on the number of managers likely to be using copied documents, or the number of documents copied annually. In return for the licence and thus legal copying, the organisation pays an annual fee to the CLA.

With the increase in the amount of documentation available electronically through computer telecommunications links, the situation threatens to become more complex before working solutions emerge to cover all working practices. Legislation has not kept pace with technology. Consequently at the time of writing, the situation is ill-defined and difficult to police.

It is unusual to find the responsibility for ensuring copyright compliance allocated to an individual within an organisation. It may be the preserve of a librarian if there is one, or the company secretary, but it is the responsibility of each individual to ensure that infringements are not made and therefore that penalties are not incurred.

Copyright checklist for internal use of copied information

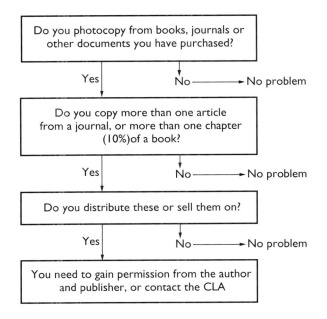

Copyright Licensing Agency Ltd, 90 Tottenham Court Rd, London, W1P 9HE. Tel. 0171 436 5931. Fax 0171 436 3986

NB It has obviously only been possible to include a small number of the many rules and regulations governing copyright here. If in any doubt, please contact the CLA for further information. It is definitely better to be safe than sorry.

Data protection

While copyright covers the copying of works produced by others, the Data Protection Act (1984) came into force to give rights to 'living and identifiable' individuals about whom information is held. However, the Act only covers information that is 'automatically processable'. This means that information held on paper in filing cabinets is **not** covered. Any information which has reference to an individual and is held on microfiche or video, for example, which is linked to a computer (i.e. automatically processable) **is** covered. This includes all the data relating to an individual held on computer. The Act obliges those who record and use data in this way on individuals to be open about that use and follow sound and proper practices. If individuals discover information about themselves, they may challenge it, and, if appropriate, claim compensation.

This can be a complex affair using, like copyright, many terms which require definition.

Exempt data
This includes personal data which is:

- Held on a home-computer for household and recreational purposes
- Used for calculating pensions and wages
- Used for distributing articles or information to data subjects
- Held by unincorporated members of a club
- Required legally to be made public (e.g. electoral roll)
- Required for purposes of national security

Caveat: Be wary of the exemptions. They are not as clear cut as they may appear.

The register

Every data user who holds personal data on others must be registered, unless the data are exempt. From information that the data user must supply to the Data Protection Registrar, the register will hold a record of the:

- Personal data held by the data user
- Purposes for which the data are used
- Sources from which the data were obtained
- People to whom the data may be disclosed
- Overseas countries to which the personal data may be transferred

The data protection principles

Registered data users must comply with the data protection principles which state that personal information shall be:

- Collected fairly and lawfully
- Only held for the lawful purposes stated
- Only used for the purposes stated in the register
- Adequate, relevant and not excessive to the purposes stated
- Accurate, up to date and not held for longer than necessary
- Accessible to the individual concerned, who, where appropriate, has the right to have information about him/herself corrected or erased
- Kept secure

Personal information

This is defined as any information relating to a living, identifiable individual. Personal information can include terms or codes which describe an individual, or details of such things as bank accounts, borrowings or job history.

Individuals' rights

If damage is caused by the loss, destruction, inaccuracy or unauthorised disclosure of personal data held by a data user, then the individual can seek compensation through the courts.

Interpreting the law

There is much doubt about interpreting the requirements of the Act. Who is, and who is not, covered by the legislation and its exemptions can be unclear. There have been a number of prosecutions under the Act, with some organisations for example, failing to re-register after the statutory three years; others have failed to register at all; others did not know they had to. Exempt data, as defined above, does leave room for doubt. Clear advice can be difficult to obtain, even for simple name and address data, and information held by clubs.

Data protection checklist

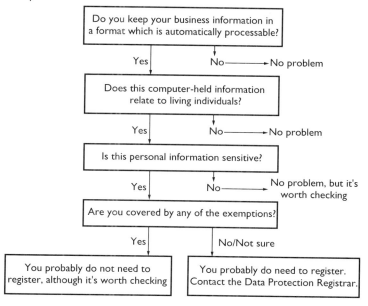

For further information, please contact the Data Protection Registrar at the address below. As with copyright, we have only been able to provide the basic facts of the Act, and we strongly recommend that any organisation holding data on individuals should be fully aware of all aspects of the Data Protection Act.

The Data Protection Registrar, Wycliffe House, Water Lane, Wilmslow, SK9 5AF. Tel. 01625 535777 Fax 01625 524510

Summary

Today, we have looked at the law in relation to the use of information. The two areas of copyright and data protection were examined. It is very important that the relevant rules and regulations are followed as an organisation could very easily break the law without realising, but ignorance is no defence.

Checkpoint: Am I complying with the law on copyright and data protection?

If in doubt – **CHECK.**